8/7/24

Victor Farmington Library
15 West Main Street
Victor, NY 14564

Horseback Riding

Cara Krenn

Lerner Publications ◆ Minneapolis

Copyright © 2025 by Lerner Publishing Group, Inc.

All rights reserved. International copyright secured. No part of this book may be reproduced, stored in a retrieval system, or transmitted in any form or by any means—electronic, mechanical, photocopying, recording, or otherwise—without the prior written permission of Lerner Publishing Group, Inc., except for the inclusion of brief quotations in an acknowledged review.

Lerner Publications Company
An imprint of Lerner Publishing Group, Inc.
241 First Avenue North
Minneapolis, MN 55401 USA

For reading levels and more information, look up this title at www.lernerbooks.com.

Main body text set in Billy Infant Regular. Typeface provided by SparkType.

Editor: Nicole Berglund **Photo Editor:** Nicole Berglund

Library of Congress Cataloging-in-Publication Data

Names: Krenn, Cara, author.
Title: Horseback riding / Cara Krenn.
Description: Minneapolis : Lerner Publications, [2025] | Series: Lightning bolt books - horse lover's library | Includes bibliographical references and index. | Audience: Ages 6-9 | Audience: Grades 2-3 | Summary: "Have you ever wondered how people ride horses? From caring for equipment to entering competitions, future equestrians will enjoy learning the ins and outs of this exciting sport"— Provided by publisher.
Identifiers: LCCN 2023035420 (print) | LCCN 2023035421 (ebook) | ISBN 9798765626078 (library binding) | ISBN 9798765628911 (paperback) | ISBN 9798765634967 (epub)
Subjects: LCSH: Horsemanship—Juvenile literature.
Classification: LCC SF309.2 .K75 2025 (print) | LCC SF309.2 (ebook) | DDC 798.2—dc23/eng/20230825

LC record available at https://lccn.loc.gov/2023035420
LC ebook record available at https://lccn.loc.gov/2023035421

Manufactured in the United States of America
1-1009872-51941-10/3/2023

Table of Contents

Special Bond — 4

Gear and Basics — 7

Learning to Ride — 12

Competitions — 16

Horseback Riding and You — 20

Fun Facts — 21

Glossary — 22

Learn More — 23

Index — 24

Special Bond

A rider holds the reins as their horse picks up speed. They reach a fence. The horse pulls up its legs, and they soar over the jump together.

People have been riding horses for many years. Before trains and planes, people rode horses to travel. Today, many people ride horses for fun and to compete.

A girl learns to ride a horse.

A rider spends a lot of time with their horse. They learn how to work together and form a special bond.

Gear and Basics

To ride a horse, you need the right gear. You need a helmet, long pants, and hard shoes with a small heel.

Horses also need gear called tack. Tack includes saddles and stirrups that help the rider stay on the horse.

A bridle, bit, and reins help the rider guide the horse.

Horseback riding includes grooming and caring for horses. New riders can read books and watch videos to learn more about horses.

An adult should be with you when you go riding. Loud noises and fast movements can scare horses.

Stay calm around horses.

Approach horses slowly.

Before you walk up to a horse, make sure it sees you. Stay near its front.

Learning to Ride

Lessons are a great way to learn to ride. Riding teachers will help you.

Balance is an important part of riding. Sit up straight in the saddle. Relax your shoulders.

Good balance helps a rider stay on their horse.

Reins tell a horse where to go.

You can learn to control your horse. It will walk when you squeeze its sides with your legs. It will stop when you say "whoa" and gently pull back on the reins.

Use the reins to turn your horse. To go right, lightly pull back on the right rein. To go left, lightly pull back on the left rein.

Competitions

After lots of riding practice, you may be ready to compete. You can learn about competitions online or from your riding teacher.

There are many ways to ride. Some riders learn how to jump over fences with their horse. This type of riding is show jumping.

A rider and her horse jump over a fence.

Different types of riding use different skills. Horses dance in a riding style called dressage.

A rider and horse perform dressage in a competition.

A cowgirl performs with a lasso in a rodeo.

Advanced riders can compete in rodeos.

No matter which kind of riding you choose, horseback riding is exciting and fun!

Horseback Riding and You

Riding is about more than skill. Riders also need to know how to care for their horses and gear. What would you most enjoy about horseback riding?

Fun Facts

- Horseback riding events are part of the Olympic Games.

- Kids race Shetland ponies at a big competition in Britain every year.

- Riding a horse without a saddle is called bareback riding.

Glossary

balance: the ability to stay on a horse

bond: relationship

dressage: a riding style where horses perform moves in a special order

gear: tools that help someone do an activity

groom: to clean and care for a horse

reins: straps connected to a horse's face that allow the rider to direct the horse

rodeo: a contest that includes calf roping and bull riding

saddle: a seat for a rider on a horse's back

stirrups: gear that helps a rider get on a horse and stay balanced

Learn More

Britannica Kids: Horseback Riding
https://kids.britannica.com/students/article/horseback-riding/633449

Ducksters: Horse
https://www.ducksters.com/animals/horse.php

Halls, Kelly Milner. *All about Horses: A Kid's Guide to Breeds, Care, Riding, and More!* Emeryville, CA: Rockridge, 2021.

Idzikowski, Lisa. *Taking Care of Your Horse.* Minneapolis: Lerner Publications, 2025.

Stamps, Caroline. *Horses & Ponies: Everything You Need to Know, from Bridles and Breeds to Jodhpurs and Jumping!* New York: DK, 2021.

US Equestrian Federation: Your First Horseback Riding Lesson
https://www.usef.org/learning-center/videos/your-first-horseback-riding-lesson

Index

bond, 6

competition, 16

dressage, 18

gear, 7-8

groom, 9

learn, 6, 9, 12, 14, 16-17

rodeo, 19

Photo Acknowledgments

Image credits: Somogyvari/Getty Images, pp. 4, 18; Lane Oatey/Blue Jean Images/Getty Images, p. 5; SeventyFour/Getty Images, p. 6; Tetra Images/Getty Images, pp. 7, 20; John M Lund Photography Inc/Getty Images, pp. 8, 20; ferrantraite/Getty Images, p. 9; MarsYu/Getty Images, p. 10; martinedoucet/Getty Images, p. 11; Tim Platt/Getty Images, p. 12; nd3000/Getty Images, p. 13; Sean Russell/Getty Images, p. 14; Eileen Groome/Getty Images, p. 15; christinepemberton/Getty Images, p. 16; Zocha_K/Getty Images, p. 17; Pete Saloutos/Getty Images, p. 19.
Cover: Adie Bush/Getty Images.

Victor Farmington Library
15 West Main Street
Victor, NY 14564